Piano • Vocal • Guitar

THE BEST BROADWAY
SONGS EVER

W9-CIX-086

HAL LEONARD
PUBLISHING
CORPORATION

Home Office: National Sales Office:
960 East Mark Street   8112 West Bluemound Road
Winona MN 55987   Milwaukee WI 53213

THE BEST BROADWAY SONGS EVER

ALL THE THINGS YOU ARE

(From "VERY WARM FOR MAY")

Words by OSCAR HAMMERSTEIN II
Music by JEROME KERN

Moderately Slowly

You are the prom-ised kiss of spring-time That makes the lone-ly win-ter seem long. _____ You are the breath-less hush of eve-ning That trem-bles on the brink of a love-ly song. _____

AND ALL THAT JAZZ
(FROM "CHICAGO")

Words by FRED EBB
Music by JOHN KANDER

ANOTHER OP'NIN', ANOTHER SHOW
(From "KISS ME, KATE")

Words and Music by
COLE PORTER

ANYONE CAN WHISTLE
(From "ANYONE CAN WHISTLE")

Words and Music by
STEPHEN SONDHEIM

BEING ALIVE
(From "COMPANY")

Words and Music by
STEPHEN SONDHEIM

AS LONG AS HE NEEDS ME

(From the Columbia Pictures - Romulus film "OLIVER!")

Words and Music by LIONEL BART

WHERE IS LOVE?
(From the Columbia Pictures — Romulus film "OLIVER!")

Words and Music by
LIONEL BART

Slowly, but rhythmically

Where _____ is love? Does it fall from skies a - bove?

Is it un-der-neath the wil - low tree_ that I've been dream - ing of?

Where _____ is she who I close my eyes to see?

BESS, YOU IS MY WOMAN
(From "PORGY AND BESS")

Words by DUBOSE HEYWARD and IRA GERSHWIN
Music by GEORGE GERSHWIN

Bess, You Is My Wo-man now, _____ You is, _____ You is! An'
you mus' laugh an' sing an' dance for two in-stead of one. _____ Want no
wrin-kle on yo' brow no-how, be-cause de sor-row of the past is all done,

I GOT PLENTY O' NUTTIN'
(From "PORGY AND BESS")

Words by IRA GERSHWIN
and DuBOSE HEYWARD
Music by GEORGE GERSHWIN

SUMMERTIME
(From "PORGY AND BESS")

Words by DuBOSE HEYWARD
Music by GEORGE GERSHWIN

BEWITCHED

(From "PAL JOEY")

Words by LORENZ HART
Music by RICHARD RODGERS

Chorus 3: Sweet again, Petite again, And on my proverbial seat again.
Be-witched, both-ered and be-wil-dered am I.
What am I? Half shot am I. To think that he loves me, So hot am I.
Be-witched, both-ered and be-wil-dered am I.
Though at first we said "No, sir."
Now we're two lit-tle dears.
You might say we are clos-er
Than Roe-buck is to Sears.
I'm dumb a-gain And numb a-gain, A rich, read-y, ripe lit-tle plum a-gain.
Be-witched, both-ered and be-wil-dered am I.

BROADWAY BABY
(From "FOLLIES")

Words and Music by
STEPHEN SONDHEIM

BY STRAUSS
(From "THE SHOW IS ON")

Words by IRA GERSHWIN
Music by GEORGE GERSHWIN

CABARET
(From the Musical "CABARET")

Music by JOHN KANDER
Words by FRED EBB

cab - a - ret. _____ ret. Come taste the

wine, Come hear the band, Come blow the horn, start

cel - e - brat - ing, Right this way, your ta - ble's wait - ing. { No use per -
{ Start by ad -

mit - ting some proph - et of doom _____ To wipe ev - 'ry smile a -
mit - ting from cra - dle to tomb _____ is - n't that long a

I LOVED YOU ONCE IN SILENCE
(From "CAMELOT")

Words by Alan Jay Lerner
Music by Frederick Loewe

CAMELOT
(From "CAMELOT")

Words by ALAN JAY LERNER
Music by FREDERICK LOEWE

IF EVER I WOULD LEAVE YOU

(From "CAMELOT")

Words by Alan Jay Lerner
Music by Frederick Loewe

Intro: Moderately

CLIMB EV'RY MOUNTAIN

(From "THE SOUND OF MUSIC")

Words by OSCAR HAMMERSTEIN II
Music by RICHARD RODGERS

THE SOUND OF MUSIC
(From "THE SOUND OF MUSIC")

Words by OSCAR HAMMERSTEIN II
Music by RICHARD RODGERS

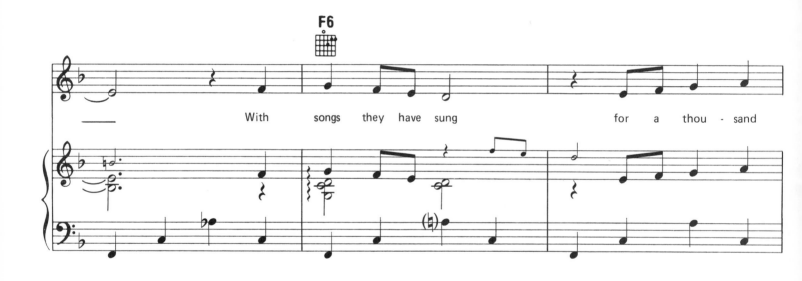

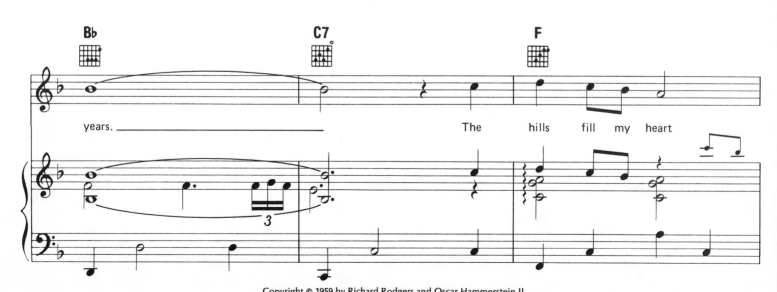

with the sound of mu - sic. _____ My heart wants to sing ev'-ry song it hears. _____ My heart wants to beat like the wings of the birds that rise from the lake to the trees. My heart wants to sigh like a

MY FAVORITE THINGS
(From "THE SOUND OF MUSIC")

Words by OSCAR HAMMERSTEIN II
Music by RICHARD RODGERS

COMEDY TONIGHT
(From "A FUNNY THING HAPPENED ON THE WAY TO THE FORUM")

Words and Music by
STEPHEN SONDHEIM

DON'T CRY FOR ME ARGENTINA

(From The Opera "EVITA")

Lyric by TIM RICE
Music by ANDREW LLOYD WEBBER

It won't be ea-sy, you'll think it strange   When I

PEOPLE

(From "FUNNY GIRL")

Words by BOB MERRILL
Music by JULE STYNE

DON'T RAIN ON MY PARADE

(From "FUNNY GIRL")

Words by BOB MERRILL
Music by JULE STYNE

Brightly

Don't tell me not to fly, I've sim-ply got to. If some-one takes a spill, it's me and not you.

Don't bring a-round a cloud To rain on my pa-rade.

Don't tell me not to live, just sit and put-ter. Life's can-dy and the sun's a ball of but-ter.

EVERYTHING'S COMING UP ROSES
(From "GYPSY")

Words by Stephen Sondheim
Music by Jule Styne

92

SMALL WORLD
(From "GYPSY")

Words by STEPHEN SONDHEIM
Music by JULE STYNE

FALLING IN LOVE WITH LOVE

(From "THE BOYS FROM SYRACUSE")

Words by LORENZ HART
Music by RICHARD RODGERS

Moderate Waltz

FROM THIS MOMENT ON
(From "OUT OF THIS WORLD")

Words and Music by COLE PORTER

Suddenly lively

Dbm   Ab   Ebm7

I need so much,___ Got the skin___ I

F7   Eb

love to touch,___ Got the arms___ to

Bb7   Eb   Guitar Tacet

hold me tight,___ Got the sweet lips___ to

Fm

kiss me good-night,___ From this mo-ment on,___

GETTING TO KNOW YOU

(From "THE KING AND I")

Words by OSCAR HAMMERSTEIN II
Music by RICHARD RODGERS

HELLO, YOUNG LOVERS
(From "THE KING AND I")

Very moderately

Words by OSCAR HAMMERSTEIN II
Music by RICHARD RODGERS

I BELIEVE IN YOU
(From "HOW TO SUCCEED IN BUSINESS WITHOUT REALLY TRYING")

Words and Music by FRANK LOESSER

GIVE MY REGARDS TO BROADWAY

(From "GEORGE M!")

Words and Music by
GEORGE M. COHAN

Give my re-gards to Broad - way, Re-

mem-ber me to Her - ald Square;_____ Tell all the

gang, at For - ty Sec - ond Street that I will soon be

(I'M A)
YANKEE DOODLE DANDY
(From "GEORGE M!")

Words and Music by
GEORGE M. COHAN

HOW ARE THINGS IN GLOCCA MORRA

(From "FINIAN'S RAINBOW")

Words by E.Y. HARBURG
Music by BURTON LANE

LOOK TO THE RAINBOW

(From "FINIAN'S RAINBOW")

Words by E.Y. HARBURG
Music by BURTON LANE

I COULD HAVE DANCED ALL NIGHT
(From "MY FAIR LADY")

Words by ALAN JAY LERNER
Music by FREDERICK LOEWE

On the Street Where You Live

(From "MY FAIR LADY")

Words by ALAN JAY LERNER
Music by FREDERICK LOEWE

I'VE GROWN ACCUSTOMED TO HER FACE

(From "MY FAIR LADY")

Words by ALAN JAY LERNER
Music by FREDERICK LOEWE

WOULDN'T IT BE LOVERLY

(From "MY FAIR LADY")

Words by ALAN JAY LERNER
Music by FREDERICK LOEWE

I'LL BE SEEING YOU
(From "RIGHT THIS WAY")

Words and Music by IRVING KAHAL
and SAMMY FAIN

I REMEMBER IT WELL

(From "GIGI")

Words by ALAN JAY LERNER
Music by FREDERICK LOEWE

IF I RULED THE WORLD

(From "PICKWICK")

Words by LESLIE BRICUSSE
Music by CYRIL ORNADEL

IF I LOVED YOU
(From "CAROUSEL")

Words by OSCAR HAMMERSTEIN II
Music by RICHARD RODGERS

YOU'LL NEVER WALK ALONE
(From "CAROUSEL")

Words by OSCAR HAMMERSTEIN II
Music by RICHARD RODGERS

IF I WERE A RICH MAN
(From the Musical "FIDDLER ON THE ROOF")

Words by SHELDON HARNICK
Music by JERRY BOCK

SUNRISE, SUNSET
(From the Musical "FIDDLER ON THE ROOF")

Words by SHELDON HARNICK
Music by JERRY BOCK

Moderately Slow Waltz Tempo
(soulful and wistful)

Is this the lit-tle boy I car - ried? Is this the lit-tle girl at
Now is the lit-tle boy a bride - groom, Now is the lit-tle girl a

play?
bride.

I don't re - mem-ber grow-ing old - er,
Un - der the can-o-py I see them,

When did they?_____
Side by side._____

When did she get to be a
Place the gold ring a - round her

IT'S ALL RIGHT WITH ME

(From "CAN-CAN")

Words and Music by
COLE PORTER

IT MIGHT AS WELL BE SPRING

(From "STATE FAIR")

Words by OSCAR HAMMERSTEIN II
Music by RICHARD RODGERS

JUST IN TIME
(From "BELLS ARE RINGING")

Words by BETTY COMDEN and ADOLPH GREEN
Music by JULE STYNE

Intro: Moderately

THE LADY IS A TRAMP
(From "BABES IN ARMS")

Words by LORENZ HART
Music by RICHARD RODGERS

MY FUNNY VALENTINE

(From "BABES IN ARMS")

Words by LORENZ HART
Music by RICHARD RODGERS

WHERE OR WHEN
(From "BABES IN ARMS")

Words by LORENZ HART
Music by RICHARD RODGERS

LUCK BE A LADY
(From "GUYS AND DOLLS")

Words and Music by
FRANK LOESSER

OL' MAN RIVER
(From "SHOW BOAT")

Words by OSCAR HAMMERSTEIN II
Music by JEROME KERN

MAKE BELIEVE
(From "SHOW BOAT")

Words by OSCAR HAMMERSTEIN II
Music by JEROME KERN

OKLAHOMA
(From "OKLAHOMA!")

Words by OSCAR HAMMERSTEIN II
Music by RICHARD RODGERS

O—k-la-hom-a, Ev-'ry night my hon-ey lamb and I———— sit a-lone and talk and watch a hawk mak-in' laz-y cir-cles in the sky.———— We know we be-long to the land————

OH, WHAT A BEAUTIFUL MORNIN'
(From "OKLAHOMA!")

Words by OSCAR HAMMERSTEIN II
Music by RICHARD RODGERS

PEOPLE WILL SAY WE'RE IN LOVE

(From "OKLAHOMA!")

Words by OSCAR HAMMERSTEIN II
Music by RICHARD RODGERS

MEMORY
(From "CATS")

Text by TREVOR NUNN after T.S. ELIOT
Music by ANDREW LLOYD WEBBER

morn - ing___ Day - light.___ I must wait for the sun - rise,___ I must think of a

new life___ And I must-n't give in._____ When the dawn comes to - night will be a

mem-o - ry too___ And a new day___ will___ be - gin.

Burnt out ends of smok - y days___ the stale cold smell of___

MY CUP RUNNETH OVER

(From "I DO! I DO!")

Words by TOM JONES
Music by HARVEY SCHMIDT

NOT A DAY GOES BY
(From "MERRILY WE ROLL ALONG")

Words and Music by
STEPHEN SONDHEIM

Not A Day Goes By, ___ not a sin-gle day
Not A Day Goes By, ___ not a sin-gle day

you're not some-where a part of my life ___ and I need you to stay
but you're some-where a part of my life ___ and it looks like you'll stay

ON A CLEAR DAY
(YOU CAN SEE FOREVER)

(From "ON A CLEAR DAY YOU CAN SEE FOREVER")

Words by ALAN JAY LERNER
Music by BURTON LANE

SEPTEMBER SONG
(From the Musical Play "KNICKERBOCKER HOLIDAY")

Words by MAXWELL ANDERSON
Music by KURT WEILL

SEVENTY SIX TROMBONES
(From "THE MUSIC MAN")

By MEREDITH WILLSON

Sev - en - ty six trom - bones led the big pa - rade,_____ with a hun - dred and ten cor - nets close at hand._____ They were fol - lowed by rows and rows of the

bat - ter - y,_____ Thun - der - ing, thun - der - ing, loud - er than be -

fore. Clar - i - nets of ev - 'ry size and trum - pet - ers who'd im - pro - vise a

full oc - tave high - er than the score.

Sev - en - ty six trom -

TILL THERE WAS YOU

(From "THE MUSIC MAN")

By MEREDITH WILLSON

SMOKE GETS IN YOUR EYES
(From "ROBERTA")

Words by OTTO HARBACH
Music by JEROME KERN

SEND IN THE CLOWNS

(From the musical "A LITTLE NIGHT MUSIC")

Music and Lyrics by STEPHEN SONDHEIM

SOME ENCHANTED EVENING
(From "SOUTH PACIFIC")

Words by OSCAR HAMMERSTEIN II
Music by RICHARD RODGERS

THIS NEARLY WAS MINE
(From "SOUTH PACIFIC")

Words by OSCAR HAMMERSTEIN II
Music by RICHARD RODGERS

Moderately

YOUNGER THAN SPRINGTIME
(From "SOUTH PACIFIC")

Words by OSCAR HAMMERSTEIN II
Music by RICHARD RODGERS

TRY TO REMEMBER
(From "THE FANTASTICKS")

Words by TOM JONES
Music by HARVEY SCHMIDT

Slowly, with tenderness

WHAT KIND OF FOOL AM I?
(From the Musical Production "STOP THE WORLD - I WANT TO GET OFF")

Words and Music by
LESLIE BRICUSSE
and ANTHONY NEWLEY

WHO CAN I TURN TO
(When Nobody Needs Me)
(From the Musical Production "THE ROAR OF THE GREASEPAINT - THE SMELL OF THE CROWD")

Words and Music by LESLIE BRICUSSE
and ANTHONY NEWLEY

Slowly with expression

Who can I turn to _____ when no-bod-y needs me? _____

My heart wants to know and so I must go where

des - ti - ny leads me. _____ With no star to guide me,